ISBN 978-1-5285-1670-9
PIBN 10906186

1 MONTH OF
FREE
READING

at

www.ForgottenBooks.com

By purchasing this book you are eligible for one month membership to ForgottenBooks.com, giving you unlimited access to our entire collection of over 1,000,000 titles via our web site and mobile apps.

To claim your free month visit:

www.forgottenbooks.com/free906186

English
Français
Deutsche
Italiano
Español
Português

www.forgottenbooks.com

Mythology Photography **Fiction**
Fishing Christianity **Art** Cooking
Essays Buddhism Freemasonry
Medicine **Biology** Music **Ancient**
Egypt Evolution Carpentry Physics
Dance Geology **Mathematics** Fitness
Shakespeare **Folklore** Yoga Marketing
Confidence Immortality Biographies
Poetry **Psychology** Witchcraft
Electronics Chemistry History **Law**
Accounting **Philosophy** Anthropology
Alchemy Drama Quantum Mechanics
Atheism Sexual Health **Ancient History**
Entrepreneurship Languages Sport
Paleontology Needlework Islam
Metaphysics Investment Archaeology
Parenting Statistics Criminology
Motivational

MADE IN CANADA

THE SUMMIT OF PAPER QUALITY

THE CREST

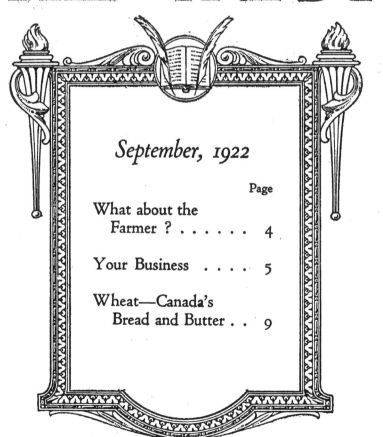

September, 1922

HOWARD SMITH PAPER MILLS
LIMITED

HE principal trouble with the easy-going fellow is that it's so hard to get him started.—Ex.

THE CREST

Vol. II   SEPT., 1922   No. 4

AUTUMN

E'RE just at the corner of autumn, with all its riot and glory of colour.

We're stepping into another season—for some a period of accomplishment because they were ready; for others a period of preparation for future conquests and for all of us a reminder that we might have planned more thoroughly and worked with greater vigour. The present is a day of reckoning for the past.

The seasons roll around—there are only four—then we find ourselves launched into another year.

Prosperity follows depression as depression succeeds prosperity.

One cycle merges into the next and business records become commercial history.

It's never too early to plan and prepare—it's often too late to mend and profit.

WHERE DO YOU STAND?

HETHER he wishes it or not, the present is a challenge to a man's right to rule in business. Also, it is an opportunity.

With men on every hand—old-timers, as well as new—vacillating under the stress of mixed emotions, subject to the fears of the wilderness ahead, there is an opportunity for the courageous, the far-seeing, the man with sound judgment and a definite ambition, to take advantage of the present conditions and gain a long march on his contemporaries. It is being done. New leaders in men and business concerns are in the making.

Old concerns that have adopted a stand-pat policy, that are awaiting business recovery before they shall strive for business, are likely, when that time comes, to find others in the field so soundly entrenched as to make the doing of business by the stand-patters doubly difficult.

See the new names in the advertising columns of the magazines, newspapers, trade journals. See the new selling organizations that have suddenly sprung up, tuned to a high pitch of enthusiasm and covering every nook and corner of the country under an aggressive sales policy that is making itself felt everywhere. They are not only getting business now, in the present, but they are also securing to themselves a position for the future that will make it hard indeed for their older competitors, who have lain low, to come back.

A man can well afford to pause and ask himself, "Where will my business be next year and five years hence?" The answer is to be found in his own mind.

Material things originate first in the mind. A house and automobile are conceived in the mind before they are built in fact. The same is true of business. Such practical things as orders, volume, profits, are the result of mental activities before physical.

The mind beset by fears, concerned only with hazards of the times, that refuses to risk in the interests of gain, cannot, by any reasonable rule of business as of life, hope to achieve that which is the goal of every business. Think twice before you decide to continue to "lay low" with your business.—*The Shur-on Chronicle.*

O to be up and doing, O!
Unfearing and unashamed to go
In all the uproar and the press
About my human business!
My undissuaded heart I hear
Whisper courage in my ear.
With voiceless calls, the ancient earth
Summons me to a daily birth.
                            —R. L. S.

WHAT ABOUT THE FARMER?

"Neath the light, by his fireside,
Planning, planning and deciding
What to buy.

*   *   *   *

It's not very far distant to the time when the farmer will be turning his six months' labours, his wheat, his oats and his crops into cash and credit.

Once his harvest is in, he plans and thinks and talks and writes letters for catalogues, booklets and information and he visits the stores in the nearby towns and cities.

Once his harvest is in he has time to read and plans form themselves into actions and then he begins to buy—and, throughout the late autumn and during the dark winter evenings, with his fireside as a friendly companion, he thinks and dreams of Spring and its needs— the replenishing of supplies here and there— the many matters calling for attention— the long-desired something which, this year, *will* be installed "without fail".

Markets for mere postage stamps. Sales will come to those who are companionable and instructive to the farmer, waiting and eager as he sits by a cracking cheerful fire, providing the messages are attractive, thorough and interesting.

"YOUR BUSINESS"

"   ND what is your business?" remarked one of those present to the latest arrival to join the group.

"Why, you might call me an Insurance Agent."

"Really", said Brown, "I'm an actuary with the Ajax. What's your Company?"

"Well, you see," replied Mr. Newcomer, "I've a Company of my own."

"Well, I *am* surprised. We seem to be entertaining a capitalist in our midst."

The passing of these remarks had more or less focussed the attention of the group on Newcomer. He, in his turn, felt that an explanation was more or less necessary.

"Perhaps I'd better explain," he began, "You all carry insurance of many and various kinds. In fact, besides the regular fire, marine and life policies, with which we are all familiar, it seems as if we could protect ourselves against any kind of loss. There has, however, been one field never touched by insurance. So, I spend my time working out protection for that field, which ranks in importance with Life and Fire and, as a matter of fact, it is sometimes more than either".

"Well, what is that? Enlighten us," spoke up one of the group.

"Markets!" replied Newcomer.

"What do you mean?"

"Simply that time and experience have proved that there is a policy which not only extends the field but actually protects against inroads on a manufacturer's market."

"Well, I'd like to buy such protection," said Henry, the Boot and Shoe man; "what do you call this policy?"

"Regular payment continuous advertising!" replied Newcomer.

"Humph!" Brown ejaculated, "that's another angle to an old story."

BY THE WAY
BY MAIL

Have you been using Sales Letters to energize the buying mood of customers; single sheet or double (with four pages): the latter giving you a chance to use colour or illustration?

*   *   *

Then, of course, Blotters and small Envelope Folders, and Inserts, along with regular mail, at no additional postage cost are quite stimulating—really, they are.

Booklets, in elaborate or simple forms, lend an opportunity to make a complete sales' effort. They are easily distributed by your Salesmen and Dealers.

* * *

Many Catalogues and Price Lists are sadly out-of-date. New issues in new form and dress are very refreshing to your customers.

* * *

But, for the all-year tonic, helpful to the building of healthful good will, through all four seasons, and year by year, the monthly house organ is unrivalled. See page 16 and read what Stevenson says.

* * *

The above and other efforts are preparatory and complementary to the man to man salesmanship effort. They sow and also they reap and co-operate most effectively with the personal sales' effort.

* * *

Lastly, and very important, there are probably many shortages in your Stationery and Office Forms supplies at this time. To order in time is to eliminate wasteful delays in routine.

IF

After seeing a business man light a cigar and flip the match thoughtlessly into a corner of his office near a waste basket, a visitor wrote the following paraphrase of one of Kipling's best known poems:—

"If you can toss a match into a clearing,
And never give a thought to put it out,
Or drop your cigarette butt without fearing,
That flames may kindle in the leaves about,
If you can knock the ashes from your brier,
Without a glance to see where they may fall,
And later find the forest all afire,
Where you have passed—with no one near to call;
If you drive your auto through the working,
And cast your stogie stub into the slash,
Unmindful of the danger therein lurking,
Or homes or happiness that you may smash;
If you can leave your campfire while 'tis glowing,
No thought of industries that it may blight,
Or of the billion saplings in the growing,
Turned into charcoal ere the coming night,
If you can start a fire beneath a brush pile
When the wind is roaring like a distant gun—
You surely should be jailed without a trial
And labelled as lunatic, my son."

—Fire Control.

These pages are printed on our "Bard of Avon"

WHEAT, our very bread and butter, represents such an important phase in Canada's economic situation that we feel that at this time when the Great Annual Movement of our crops begins to get under way that a story covering its methods and ways will be of interest to our readers. There are many points which perhaps are not understood by many people throughout our Dominion.

The moving of this large volume of grain involves a highly organized system of handling and transportation, especially as every effort is made to get the grain into a position where it can be shipped by boat before the close of navigation and, consequently, the bulk of it is brought to the terminal elevators within a limited period.

The wheat growing Provinces, Manitoba, Saskatchewan, and Alberta, are served by a system of country elevators, situated on railway lines and within reasonable distances from the wheat fields. These elevators are all licensed by the Government and the owners must file bonds with the Board of Grain Commissioners to protect customers; consequently the holders of storage tickets have for security not only the financial resources of the elevator companies but also these surety bonds. Most of these elevators are owned by large elevator

These pages are printed on our "Bard of Avon"

companies, milling companies and large farmers' co-operative companies, commonly referred to as Line Elevator Companies. In addition to these there are single elevators and small groups owned by local dealers or farmers' associations. They vary in size; but a standard elevator has a capacity of 30,000 bushels, and altogether there are of these country elevators, operating in the three provinces, approximately 3,700.

There are four methods, by which a farmer can, under the present trade conditions, dispose of his grain, namely:—

1. By selling by the load to the nearest elevator.

2. By storing his wheat in an elevator and taking a graded Storage Ticket, his grain thereby losing its identity.

3. By engaging a special bin and taking a special bin ticket, by which the identity of his grain is kept intact and the grading and dockage fixed by the Dominion Government.

4. By not using an elevator at all, by getting a car spotted at the nearest loading platform, loading his car himself, shipping it to his own order or the order of a commission firm and handling it on the usual consignment basis.

In all methods, bar the first one, the cleaning charges, (if any), interest on freight, interest on advance and drying charges, if necessary, are all payable by the farmer, and any loss in drying is also the farmer's loss.

One Car per Man

The railways distribute cars in the order of application, a car register for this purpose being held at each station. Only one car at a time in rotation is allowed to one man, irrespective of the amount of grain he may own. This applies to elevators as well as to individuals loading at the platform.

All grain is inspected in transit, en route to the terminals. The inspection points are Calgary for grain going West of that city, Duluth for bonded grain going South and Winnipeg for all grain going East. As almost all of our surplus wheat goes to the United Kingdom and to Europe, it is at Winnipeg that the bulk of the inspection work is done. Samples are taken, five or seven from each car; these samples with the number of the car are placed in a small sack and are delivered to the Inspection Department, where they are tested for grade and cleaned for dockage. Dockage is foreign matter such as dirt, seeds, etc.

There is comparatively only a short delay of the grain at Winnipeg for sampling purposes, as the men engaged at that work are experts; five men can obtain samples from a train of forty cars in about three hours and, when the number of men is increased, a train can be cleared in approximately one hour. This work goes on steadily for seven days a week, and for twenty-four hours a day. After the grain has been inspected an official certificate of grade is issued. The officer inspecting the grain knows neither the name of the owner nor the point from which it was shipped. If the owner of the grain is not satisfied with the grade given, he may ask for a re-inspection, and if after that he still thinks the grade too low, he may ask for a Survey Board. The Survey Board is appointed by the Dominion Government and their decision is final. Regarding the inspection of grain there are one hundred and sixty-five classifications of wheat and, including the coarse grain, there are two hundred and forty-six.

After the samples have been obtained from the cars at Winnipeg, the grain is taken on to the terminal elevators at Fort William or Port Arthur, four hundred miles east of Winnipeg, at the head of Lake Superior. From this point the grain can be shipped either by lake or by rail. At the terminals the grain is unloaded and weighed by Government Weigh Masters. The bill of lading issued by the railway is eventually exchanged for a Terminal Elevator Receipt. This is the document which passes from seller to buyer when trades take place on the Winnipeg Grain Exchange.

The Winnipeg Grain Exchange

In 1883 an attempt to form a Grain Exchange failed, and it was not until 1887 that the Winnipeg Grain and Produce Exchange was opened. It was incorporated in 1891 by Act of the Manitoba Legislature, but because of certain adverse legislation it was dissolved, and there was organized the present Winnipeg Grain Exchange as a voluntary non-incorporated association. As such it is a self governing institution; it is independent of any charter and, as such, it has operated from 1908 till now. This is the largest "Cash" Wheat Market in the world.

The Association as such neither buys nor sells, it does not trade in grain at all and it does not fix prices. It is only an association of grain dealers whose objects are to secure information, to provide a suitable meeting place and to establish and maintain reasonable and proper terms and regulations for the prompt and efficient making and performance of contracts.

The "Cash" price is for grain in store at a terminal elevator; "Track" price is for grain loaded in a car at a country point and "Street" price is for grain in waggon lots at a country point. The value of wheat depends on its relative position to the market, so it naturally follows that cash or spot wheat commands the highest price.

The sellers of cash grain on the Exchange include the elevator companies, farmers' associations and commission men, all of whom are acting on behalf of the producer. The buyers include Canadian millers and exporters selling to British or European mills, either direct or through other channels. It follows, we think, that true competitive prices are fairly established.

Our surplus wheat is exported and the price paid in Winnipeg is the price paid by the foreign buyer less freight from Fort William to destination, insurance and the seller's profit.

The building in which the Exchange operates is the largest office building in Winnipeg, and is occupied almost entirely by grain firms.

Cash wheat refers to the purchase and sale of actual grain. Purchases made under a future market contract may be delivered on any day of the month designated at the option of the seller. The buyer consequently has no guarantee that he will be tendered the grain before the end of the month. Contracts from foreign buyers do not necessarily fit in with this delivery date and the exporter may require the wheat, say, on the 20th of the month. Consequently he has to go out and buy the cash wheat. This situation obtains in regard to all shippers, and immediately there is created a competitive buying for the actual grain; naturally prices go up and a premium is offered over the future price. These premiums vary constantly, being regulated by supply and demand. Within the past eighteen months premiums as high as twenty-five cents a bushel were paid for cash wheat.

It is not usual for the buyer and seller to negotiate direct, this being done by Cash Grain Brokers, nor are cash grain transactions executed in the pit. When the sale is made the deal is completed in a very simple manner—the seller on receipt of payment hands the buyer a terminal warehouse receipt for the amount and grade purchased. When the shipper wants the grain shipped he hands his warehouse receipt to the Lake Shippers' Clearance Association who attend to all details, and when the boat or car is loaded they return to him (the shipper) or his nominee, the lake or rail bills of lading. The exporter or miller thus completes the entire transaction without at any time seeing a kernel of the grain. The Canadian system of grading is looked upon by the foreign buyers with such favor that a dispute regarding the quality of the wheat is almost unknown. This does not, of course, necessarily apply to what is sold on sample. In such a case a dispute would be settled by a Board of Arbitration.

Summary by Courtesy of The Royal Bank Magazine.

(*To be continued*).

TWO REAL PROBLEMS

HERE are two important problems which confront every business to-day. One is to get customers; the other, how to hold old customers. Both are of equal importance.

Business men have been known who would spend five hundred dollars in travelling expenses in order to get a new customer and never give the expenditure a second thought; and yet, the next day, would curtly refuse to make a fifty-cent adjustment asked by an old customer.

The old customer might quit. "A matter of principle," the boss would say; but—if a new customer is worth five hundred dollars, isn't an old one worth fifty cents?

The trouble with many of us is that when we get into business, we think we no longer have a boss. The fact is that a man working for someone else has one boss, while the man in business has as many bosses as he has customers.

The old adage, "The customer is always right," is the better policy.—*Sparks*.

What you know is a club for yourself and what you don't know is a meat-axe for the other fellow.—*G. H. Lorimer.*

* * *

Blessed are they who were not satisfied to let well enough alone. All that the world is to-day we owe to them.—*Nuggets.*

* * *

The bitterness of low quality lasts long after the sweetness of low price has been forgotten.
—*Roe Fulkerson, in the Fellow Worker.*

* * *

Only a watch repairer can keep his eye on a timepiece and still tend to business.—*Ex.*

* * *

"And am I the only girl you have ever—" "Wait a minute, Molly. Before you ask me that, do you want me to lie and flatter you, or tell you the truth and satisfy your curiosity?"
—*Richmond Times-Dispatch.*

ANOTHER GOOD REASON FOR HOUSE ORGANS

If a man but talk of himself in the right spirit; refers to his virtuous actions by the way and never applies to them the name of virtue, how easily his evidence is accepted in the Court of Public Opinion—*R. Louis Stevenson.*

These pages are printed on our "Bard of Avon"

Bard of Avon

is manufactured
in two weights
in White and
Toned, and in
Laid and Wove.

also

Bard of Avon

Cover

Wove Only
White & Toned

OUR
SERVICE
DEPARTMENT

exists to help you
make money out of
your paper expendi-
tures devoted to
advertising, and to
suggest ways to save
money without sac-
rifice of necessary
quality in the paper
you use for your
daily and routine
requirements

*Send us samples of your
printing and ask us
questions*

Where should I use it?

Many readers, who have not given much study to the economical use of paper, may desire to answer to this question.

is a tub-sized, loft dried paper made in White and Seven Colours especially adapted to the following specific uses:

Letterheads, Sales Letters

Ledger Sheets, Insurance Policies

Invoice and Statement Forms

and all forms requiring a good strong paper

Bell-Fast is also made as a Ledger Paper, watermarked in the style as above, "Bell-Fast Ledger"

Your request, accompanied by samples, will enable us to suggest proper paper specifications for you needs.

MADE IN CANADA

CPSIA information can be obtained
at www.ICGtesting.com
Printed in the USA
BVHW071714280119
538842BV00035B/4485/P

9 781528 516709